LIVING

A

LIFE OF PURPOSE

**ELIMINATING DISTRACTIONS TO
ACCOMPLISH GOD'S PURPOSE FOR YOUR LIFE**

ROSELINE
UWAIFO

CAPTIVES FREE
PUBLISHING HOUSE

Living a life of purpose

This book is a gift

to

_____

from

_____

on the occasion of

_____

Date

_____

Your journey into living a purposeful life has just begun

Living a life of purpose

Books by Roseline Uwaifo

Who is God to you?

Discovering Marriage and Family Uniqueness

Living a life of purpose

LIVING A LIFE OF PURPOSE
Copyright © 2020 by Roseline Uwaifo

Captives Free Publishing House,
86 Townsfield Road
Westhoughton,
BL5 2PA
Bolton.
Email: pastormrsuwaifo@gmail.com.
Tel: Within United Kingdom. 07787543569
Outside United Kingdom 0044-7787543569

Unless otherwise stated, all Scripture quotations are taken from the Holy Bible, New Living Translation (NLT). Other versions cited are NIV, NKJV, AMP, and KJV. Quotations marked NIV are taken from the HOLY BIBLE, NEW INTERNATIONAL VERSION. Copyright © 1973, 1978, 1984 by International Bible Society. Used by permission of Hodder and Stoughton Ltd, a member of the Hodder Headline Plc Group. All rights reserved. "NIV" is a registered trademark of the International Bible Society. UK trademark number 1448790. Quotations marked KJV are from the Holy Bible, King James Version.

Ordering Information: Quantity sales. For details, contact the publisher at the address above. Printed in the United Kingdom.

Publisher's Cataloging-in-Publication data
Uwaifo, Roseline.
Living a Life of Purpose/ Roseline Uwaifo
ISBN 978-0-9931599-2-3
The main category of the book — Faith

First Edition

Dedication

I dedicate this book to the Almighty God, and the Lord of my soul who gave His son, Jesus Christ of Nazareth, to die for mankind. I will forever praise His Name.

Contents

Living a life of purpose

Acknowledgments

I acknowledge Rev and Rev (Mrs) Omoregie for their sincere commitment to helping others succeed in their vision. Thanks for your care and support during my challenges. I am blessed to have you in my life.

I greatly appreciate my children Angel and Godswill Uwaifo for keeping strong in faith during the challenges of our lives. And to my Heaven made husband late Mr. Osahon Uwaifo. You will always be in our hearts. "we love you dad always" says your children Angel and Godswill Uwaifo.

I am grateful to my mentor Mrs. Kathleen Naeem, a widow with a great love for everyone that comes her way. Mama Kathleen, as I call her, thanks for being there for me whenever I needed motherly encouragement as a widow. May you live long to be appreciated in Jesus Mighty Name.

I am also grateful Dirk and Sylvia Vierbaum in Germany. These are Germans with a passion for widows and people in need. You are a couple with a heart for God. May God's name be praised in your lives for your care and support for me and family in Jesus Mighty name.

To Pastor Loveday Uyi Evbuomwan (The Narrow Gate Foursquare Church, Italy), thanks for your encouraging words and care for my family. Your family is blessed forever in Jesus' Mighty Name.

My special thanks go to Pastor Edmund Abekhe (RCCG), a member of the trustee to New Life in Christ Evangelical Ministry (The New Jerusalem). Thanks for your stand in the Ministry. You are one in a million. Pastor Tunji Ogedengbe of a DTT Consultancy Limited, I will always appreciate you for your service and support. You are blessed in Jesus Mighty Name

My uncompromised love goes to the late Mr. and Mrs. Sunday Omokaro. And to all the children which I am privileged to be one of them, may the Almighty God continue to keep us all in Jesus' Mighty Name.

To all members of New Life in Christ Evangelical Ministry (Leigh), I am grateful for your support. The good Lord will perform great miracles in your life in Jesus' Mighty Name.

Special to thanks to Opeyemi Farinde for taking my writing ministry to the next level. May God's Holy Name be praised in your life in Jesus' Mighty Name.

Preface

For by him were all things created, that are in heaven, and that are in earth, visible and invisible, whether they be thrones, or dominions, or principalities, or powers: all things were created by him, and for him – Colossians 1:16 KJV.

The writing of this book is based on my encounter with God. My experience with God comes through dreams and deep meditation on the Word of God. Early in life, I did not consider myself a writer because I felt a writer must have a special skill. But by the move of God in my life through the leading of the Holy Spirit, I became aware that one of the most potent ways to reach out to the people of the world is by writing divinely inspired books. Therefore, writing inspirational books is an essential task God gave me to achieve purpose in life.

Writing this book is one of my life's testimonies and sharing my knowledge with you is achieving God's purpose for my life. I hope this book inspires you to seek God for the achievement of His purpose for your life. When God calls you, your response has a lot to do with fulfilling destiny.

To achieve a purpose in life, you need to cut out distraction. Growing up, God told me it was important I keep distractions away from my life and focus on Him. Despite this audible instruction from God, I could not easily deal with many of the distractions that try to derail me from the plans of God for my life. But by the Grace of God, I was realigned to His original path for me.

To leverage on the Grace of God requires that I become deliberate about dealing with the distractions in my life. You may not even easily recognize that you are distracted. But when you are deliberate about spotting distractions and dealing with them, you begin to move according to God's divine agenda for your life.

God created the world and everything in it to accomplish His purpose. Being alive is part of God's divine agenda for your life.

God knows everything from the beginning to the end and He is familiar with his creation. The word of God reveals in Colossians 1 verse 16 that *"all things were created by Him and for Him."* God created the heaven and the earth, principality, and power.

When we talk about what God created and the situations and experiences around us, we attempt to question God. Among the common questions we ask are: Why did God create me like this? Why did God allow me to go through these situations and mess? But if we realize that God created heaven and earth, then He has power over everything. He has the power to kill and to make alive. When we recognize God as the ultimate creator, we allow him to walk us through the process we feel will consume us. And when we come out of the messy situation, we gain the understanding that all that happens to us is for our good. God created all things for the manifestation of His purpose for our lives.

In God's kingdom, everyone has been given a place to serve and to accomplish a purpose. And you should not allow material things and life's circumstances affect your walk with Christ. You should not mix your fellowship with Jesus Christ with the pleasures of this world. Instead, put off falsehood and put on the armor of truth which is Jesus Christ. In John 14 verse 16, Jesus reaffirms his position as the savior of mankind as the Way, the Truth, and the Life. Without Jesus Christ, no man can see God.

Many believers around the world today are responding to God's call in different ways. Proverbs 14 verse 12 says *"There is a way which seemeth right unto a man, but the end thereof are the ways of death."* The ways of death are preceded by a materialistic or carnal way of life. Despite the successes that many have recorded in business and career, happiness is still far from their lives. Unfortunately, many people mistake success for purpose. Those who follow God faithfully are honored by God.

Anything we acquire that God has not given to us brings along trouble. Satan is attacking the destiny of many through the choice they make. The power to make a choice has been given to you by God and how you use your power of choice determines your destiny. Many are afflicted today by their wrong choice. Your destiny is solely determined by your proper or improper use of your power of choice. Believers who do not set their eyes on things above where Jesus Christ seats will look down to Satan who will mess their purpose.

Furthermore, as you take seriously fulfilling God's purpose for your life, you must be ready to eliminate detractors. To eliminate, according to the Merriam-Webster dictionary, means to remove from further consideration or competition, especially by defeat in a contest. The devil is your number one detractor and he has no good part to play in your life. You must, therefore, make one wise decision regarding your life by following Jesus, the son of God, wholeheartedly because it is through Him you can fully dominate the devil.

Finally, this book contains powerful prayer points that will align you with God's purpose for your life. Matthew 11:12 says *"And from the days of John the Baptist until now the kingdom of heaven suffers violence, and the violent take it by force."* It is your responsibility to take what belongs to you through the force of prayer. Prayer is your infallible communication channel to God. Matthew 7:7 says, *"Ask and it shall be given you!"* Prayer is a tool and weapon you can use to fire and destroy every plot of the devil without physical combat. Martin Luther says, *"prayer is the necessary breath of a Christian"* and to be a Christian without prayer is to be alive without breathing. John Calvin says, *"if prayer is of no account to us, that is sure that we are unbelievers, however much we claim to believe the gospel."* In this book, I reflected on my life's experiences and showed how I have been able to achieve God's purpose. I am confident that this book will help you in your Christian race.

Introduction

❦

*I*will praise thee; for I am fearfully and wonderfully made: marvelous are thy works; and that my soul knoweth right well – Psalm 139:14 KJV.

Everyone born of a woman is born to accomplish a specific purpose in life. Life gives what it wants to and not what you desire. If you can discover your purpose, you can accomplish and acclimatize to God's desire for you. Many in the world today just exist and are not living a life of purpose. Living without purpose is living without destiny and it is disastrous.

Purpose is a plan that gives you direction; it can be likened to a layout showing you when to turn left or right. Those who follow the advice of the wicked or hang around sinners will find it difficult to accomplish God's divine purpose for them. Psalms 1 and verses 1 and 2 says *"Blessed is the man that walketh not in the counsel of the ungodly, nor standeth in the way of sinners, nor sitteth in the seat of the scornful. But his delight is in the law of the LORD, and in his law doth he meditate day and night."*

God is the creator of purpose, and it is He alone who empowers one to accomplish it. Anyone who intends to help God in the fulfillment of purpose will work against God's divine will. It is until an individual repents from sinful acts and pleads God's mercy and forgiveness can purpose be fulfilled.

God is not happy with a sinful person. Sinful acts like disobedience to God's Word expressed through anger, bitterness, unforgiveness, unbelief, hypocrisy, malice, deceit etc. prevent you from acclimatizing to God's purpose for our lives. You need to make up your mind about God by asking Him to help you do away with sinful acts and focus on Him alone for direction. The help is available through the redemptive power of Jesus Christ.

Are you struggling in life? Is your current situation making you think of giving up on God and His purpose for your life? Do you thirst for a new life in Christ? There are answers to these questions of your heart only if you allow God to work through you as you navigate through life.

One

My Story

Through personal encounters with God in dreams and visions, I have built an intimate relationship with God to work in the area of my divine calling. In my relationship with God, I have come to the discovery that acquiring material things is not equal to achieving a purpose. This was not known to me until I eliminated distractions and focused on God's divine purpose for my life.

Distractions are elements that shift your attention from what is important. From my experience, anything can take the form of distraction when it takes the place of importance in your life. It can even relegate more important aspects of your life. A distraction can be subtle that it does not present itself as what it truly is, but you find yourself grappling with it. You have little or no control over what distracts you in life. Distraction can be something you see or not and expressed in the physical, emotional, and spiritual dimensions.

I have had people in my life who do not see anything good in what I do. They always find fault in me and talk me down.

When God called me into ministry, many people said a lot of negative things to me that distracted me from the assignment God gave me. When I lost my focus on God, I lost my self-esteem and became intimidated by people and the situations I could easily wade through. Heeding to God's call became difficult.

My experience so far in life shows that in your work with God, you would meet a lot of people along the way. Some of the people you meet will attempt to pull you down, but some will raise you in your ministry. You need to know how to deal with people who are bent on pulling you down.

My main distractions in life were wrong choices and negative words. These distractions manifested through the people I interacted with. Making the wrong choice was the most dangerous thing that happened to me. I thought I was immune to it until I found myself in the realm of the wrong choice.

Many people seem to have a false impression that they are immune to the realities of life especially if you are from a family of great material wealth. You will make a wrong choice by embracing this lie. One of the wrong choices I made was allowing Satan to make me live a life of unforgiveness. I was afflicted with bitterness, a sorrowful heart, and pain because it was difficult for me to get over the shock that the people I love and trust would hurt me.

Unforgiveness is a virus that kills unconscionably. This virus can come from anywhere. It can be from your spouse, children, parents, past or present relationship, church member, pastor, business partner, etc. When it became difficult to forgive the people who have hurt me, I began to study how unforgiveness can affect me and I realized that unforgiveness is one of the deadliest poisons that Satan uses against God's children.

Unforgiveness stunted my spiritual growth and hindered my capacity for a healthy relationship with God. Unforgiveness led me to chains of anger, suspicion, resentment, and fear. In scientific studies, unforgiveness has been classified as a disease, and some reputable research centers have begun to advocate for the treatment of emotional wounds because of the way it impacts how a patient might respond to medical treatment. Further insights from studies carried out by researchers like Dr. Michael Barry show that about 60 percent of all cancer patients have issues with forgiving those who have hurt them. Dr. Barry notes further that the first step in learning to forgive is to realize how much you have been forgiven by God. When you forgive, you pull down the burden of anger and hatred that is upon you.

Dealing with unforgiveness

"And be not conformed to this world: but be ye transformed by the renewing of your mind, that ye may prove what is that good, and acceptable, and perfect, will of God," Romans 12:2 KJV.

In 2009, the power of God touched my life anew and He showed me how much He loved me. During the divine encounter, God told me that I would be knowing him in a new way with the promise of an endless life of possibility. After this encounter, I saw a change in my way of thinking and my understanding of God. I began to see things thc way He desires I see them. I meditate on the Word of God and engage in in the place of prayer regularly. Forgiveness is divine and it flows through you if you accept the new life in Christ. *"Therefore if any man be in Christ, he is a new creature: old things are passed away; behold, all things are become new,"* 2 Corinthians 5:17 KJV.

I want you to understand that the people that hurt you have no idea of what they are doing to you. They try to hurt you because they have seen something special about your life. Jesus Christ knew that the people of Jerusalem did not know what they were doing at his crucifixion. This is what made him cry out to his Father to forgive them. Jesus Christ gave a perfect example of forgiveness by forgiving us while enduring the pain of the cross. The bible says *"And when they were come to the place, which is called Calvary, there they crucified him, and the malefactors, one on the right hand, and the other on the left. Then said Jesus, Father, forgive them; for they know not what they do. And they parted his raiment, and cast lots,"* Luke 23:33-34.

Forgiving those who hurt you provisions you for the forgiveness of God through his son Jesus Christ and quick answers to your prayers. Through the power of the Holy Spirit, your mind is renewed, and you enjoy abundant peace with God.

The whole idea of forgiveness is that it relies only on one person. You do not have to wait for the other person to ask for forgiveness before giving it. Other studies on the health benefits of forgiveness include a better relationship with people, a decrease in anxiety and stress, lower blood pressure, lower risk of depression, and strong immune and heart health. Marshall Jones Junior explains that we really can get all these benefits even if no one else wants to reconcile with us. Unforgiveness comes along with negative emotions and can have a remarkable negative impact on the body. But with forgiveness, the state of the body is effective to handle different kinds of diseases and ailments.

When you hold grudges, you hurt yourself. Forgiveness is not easy to give, but when you withhold it, you are opening the doors of your life to the devil to come in aggressively. You might feel justified within you for a short period by not forgiving the people who hurt you, but with time, it will turn into a deep-seated bitterness. Bitterness has a toxic effect on your heart, soul, and relationship with people around you and even with God.

Do not allow the distraction that comes with unforgiveness to steal your destiny and the vision of God for your life. God values the people He uses to accomplish His purpose. God does not discriminate when choosing who to fulfill His purpose. The purpose of God concerning mankind is to serve Him. And when God calls you, He equips and establishes you when you heed to the call. The fulfillment of purpose is knowing what God wants and passing it on. When you know what God requires of you and you do it in His way, you are fulfilling His purpose.

God has given you the free will to make your choice. Since Adam and Eve failed in Eden, God has since stopped choosing for mankind. But He is always available to help you make the right choice. God has given you the freedom to make your choice in your service to Him, and in the kind of people you allow into your life, home, and ministry.

How do you approach God? Who are your friends? Who is your business partner or colleague? Who is your associate in ministry? Who assists you? Who speaks into your life regarding your visions, dreams, marriage, or family issues? These are vital questions you need to examine in your desire to achieve God's purpose for your life.

Recommended steps out of unforgiveness

1. Try not to take things personally

Do not let what people do to you get into you. If you personalize all of life's issues, it will get into you and erode your peace of mind. Jesus Christ notes that offense will come to you, but it is your responsibility to stop it from getting into you. People who attack you are inadvertently attacking themselves.

2. Practice focusing on the positive side of things instead of the negative

Being positive in a world that is full of negativity requires discipline and dedication. Maintaining a positive attitude in a negative situation requires focus. You can have a positive attitude to people, and they reciprocate with negative energy. In such a situation, there is nothing you can do about those people especially when they are people you cannot easily break association with due to work, marriage, or family connection. You must remain positive even when their negativity appears to be overwhelming. A person of positivity possesses the power of endurance and has a firm belief that every negative or bad condition will change for good. Perseverance, longsuffering, and endurance all work together in a positive person.

3. Accept apology when given, if not given carry-on

Luther College researchers explained that apologies can help to move the forgiveness process along, but if "sorry" is a necessary condition for forgiveness, "then there will likely be fewer instances of forthcoming forgiveness for that individual."

Accept apology when given, and if it is not given carry-on. When an apology is given, accept it and forgive. However, to carry-on forgiving others when an apology is not given – in a world where people who have hurt us even attempts to justify their actions – is difficult. The problem with waiting for an apology is that the people who hurt you sometimes do not know what they have done to you, and you may have to wait for so long a time to reconcile with them, and you may never. Forgiving people is for your sake and not for the offending party. When you understand that forgiveness is divine, you will ask God to help you forgive people easily.

4. Do not try to change those who have refused change

We try to change people and feel they will treat us better when we can change them. Change comes only from the Lord. As a minister of the Word of God, I see myself as a messenger delivering God's instruction to the people. It is God who owns the message that can put it into action in the mind of those listening to it.

Meanwhile, God has given everyone the power to change themselves for good. As a Christian, you may seek the face of God to change the attitude of someone you are in close contact with. But you cannot on your own can change the person.

The power of choice

Adam and Eve made a wrong choice by eating the forbidding fruit and it costs them losing God's purpose for their lives. A wrong choice is anything that does not bring glory to God in your life. A wrong choice can be anything that keeps you away from God's presence. Life's choices direct your progress or stagnation spiritually and physically.

"I call heaven and earth to record this day against you, that I have set before you life and death, blessing and cursing: therefore choose life, that both thou and thy seed may live," Deuteronomy 30:19 KJV.

God recommends that we choose life according to the bible. God does not make a choice for us in the areas of marriage, career, etc., but we can seek knowledge through His Words. Also, having genuine two-way communication with Him through prayers helps us to make the right choice.

When we make a choice, God expects us to be accountable to Him. Your choices are yours alone. Some of us are where we are today because of the wrong or good choice we have made. A good choice leads to success, and the wrong choice leads to failure.

Galatians 6:7-8 says *"Do not be deceived: God is not mocked, for whatever one sows, that will he also reap. For the one who sows to his own flesh will from the flesh reap corruption, but the one who sows to the Spirit will from the Spirit reap eternal life."*

Joyce Meyer explains that *"wisdom always chooses to do now what it will be satisfied with later on."* The bible says in Proverbs 4:7 that *"Wisdom is the principal thing; therefore get wisdom: and with all thy getting get understanding."*

To grow in the knowledge of the Word of God, you must be dedicated to meditating upon it daily. This is the only means through which you can acquire true wisdom needed to choose a good life.

When you become filled with the Word of God, you gain a clear understanding of the issues of life. By this, you can make a wise decision, and are empowered to fulfill your destiny. You cannot blame Satan if you fail to accomplish God's purpose for your life because you are the result of the choice you make.

Living a life of purpose

Two

Beware of Detractors

*B*e careful for nothing; but in everything by prayer and supplication with thanksgiving let your requests be made known unto God — Philippians 4:6 KJV.

Many believers today are ignorant of the strategies Satan uses to bring men to their knees. The ability to discern rightly and wrongly enables you to understand events around you. Do not be ignorant of the devices of the crafty men – wicked human personality – because they are out to derail you from God's original plan. Do not let detractors stop you or even slow you down in any area of your life. A detractor attempts to disparage you and prevents your growth in the knowledge of the things of God.

Detractor could be someone close to you; a friend, spouse, or anyone you trust. Identifying your detractors and knowing how to deal with them helps you to focus on God. To deal with detractors, you need to understand the role they play in your life. You must be spiritually sensitive to understand how detractors work because they may appear genuine with their intentions. This knowledge helps you to manage your relationship with the people more effectively; increases your chance of becoming successful in what God has called you to; and builds your self-esteem.

Proverbs 4:7 says, *"wisdom is the principal thing; therefore get wisdom: and with all thy getting get understanding,"* KJV.

Furthermore, when you understand the roles of detractors in your life, you are guided by the Holy Spirit and able to make moves inspired by God. So, you do not have to rely on anyone for direction from God. When you are close to God, He speaks to you about how you should go with achieving His purpose. And if anyone (human) speaks to you, their opinion or advice should be in line with what God has shared with you beforehand.

One of the major tools used by detractors is to frustrate you and make you give in to the devil. Frustration is expressed through their anger, scathing criticism, and negative thoughts about what God has commanded you to do. Detractors transfer their negative thoughts to you in a way that will make you relinquish your divine goals. They achieve this by sowing the seeds of doubt and self-defeat in you. Negative words are seeds that surely grow into huge oak trees of doubt with roots that tear apart the foundation of your goal.

When you understand this, you become conscious of people with negative thoughts around you and put everything in place to block your mind against their negativities. There are some negative people in your life it may be difficult to cut close association with which may include your spouse or siblings, but with fasting and prayer, you can trust to God give you the wisdom and understanding to manage the situation.

Who are these detractors?
Detractors are:

1. Slanderers

Slanderers say unkind things about you at your back. They curse you and wish you were derailed from God's plan for your life. Their intention is to make you lose favor in the sight of your benefactors or whom God has laid it in their mind to support you for your achievement of divine purpose.

2. Seekers

The seekers collect information about you so that they can attack you from your weak point. They are not close to you but can see that God has placed in your hands a specific purpose and they have been sent by the devil to derail you.

3. Critics

Critics in this case are people who do not see anything good in you. They give negative remarks about what you do, and their purpose in your life is to make you lose courage and develop low self-esteem. They do everything to incapacitate you and make you see yourself incapable of fulfilling what God called you to.

4. *Finder*

Finders are like seekers collecting information about you to attack you from your weak spot. They are people close to you. They could be families or friends or work colleagues. Finders are inspired by the devil to monitor your progress and shift your focus from God.

5. *Competitors*

Competitors are people monitoring your life to know if you have progressed than where they are. They are more concerned about being ahead of you. And when you are not sensitive, you may derail from God's path for you by trying to prove to your competitors that you are better than them.

6. *Schemers*

Schemers are also devil inspired people using all forms of approach to shift your focus from God and His plan. They can orchestrate situations to make you think it is God working things out, whereas it is schemers shaping events around you to make you lose focus.

However, detractors are unavoidable in life, and Christians should see them as an element of life that keeps them on guard to remain spiritually sensitive. Christ even instructed Christians not to hate detractors/enemies but to pray for them. God allows detractors in your life for His own glory and this is one of the reasons you must not hate detractors.

The gains of life come through enduring a period of persistent pain. Where there is no problem, there is neither purpose nor promotion. I have come to the realization that the benefits that come with dealing with detractors in accordance with the Scriptures are much.

Have you been called foolish or given a name that does not belong to you? Have you been mocked by the people you call personal friends? Have you been betrayed by your loved ones? Have you been sold out for the selfish gains of another? Well, if that is your story, congratulation! You are on the Lord's side if you are genuinely born again, and I am confident that Jesus is working things out for your good.

Jesus Christ story – John 13:21-27 KJV
This book of the bible is written by one of the beloved disciples of Jesus Christ, Apostle John, who is also one of the sons of Zebedee. Apostle John tells us what

Jesus Christ went through to fulfil His divine purpose while here on earth.

"When Jesus had thus said, he was troubled in spirit, and testified, and said, Verily, verily, I say unto you, that one of you shall betray me. Then the disciples looked one on another, doubting of whom he spake. Now there was leaning on Jesus' bosom one of his disciples, whom Jesus loved. Simon Peter therefore beckoned to him, that he should ask who it should be of whom he spake. He then lying on Jesus' breast saith unto him, Lord, who is it? Jesus answered, He it is, to whom I shall give a sop, when I have dipped it. And when he had dipped the sop, he gave it to Judas Iscariot, the son of Simon. And after the sop Satan entered into him. Then said Jesus unto him, That thou doest, do quickly."

If you are worried that detractors are all around you and scheming to pull you down, unfortunately, you cannot stop the enemy from manifesting their evil and sinful nature. A look at the life of Jesus reveals that a Christian cannot live without a detractor. Judas was out to stop Jesus from fulfilling His purpose. Jesus gave His life for us as a good shepherd, demonstrating His greatest act of love. The wicked may prosper and increase in material possession but you should not envy them at any time.

You should take solace in the Word of God that says that the end of wickedness and every form of evil is destruction. No matter what the righteous may go through in life, he will have a great and enduring peace in the end. You should, therefore, put on your breastplate of righteousness and shun the wicked to fulfill God's purpose for our life.

Self-control

Many Christian today are selling themselves to Satan and his agent because of a lack of self-control. The lack of self-control is the consequence of making a wrong choice. Self-control is established by the Holy Spirit to help us navigate through life triumphantly. The Word of God says, *"But the fruit of the Spirit is love, joy, peace, patience, kindness, goodness, faithfulness, gentleness, self-control; against such things there is no law,"* Galatians 5:22-23 (ESV).

The Holy Spirit is the third person in God's head which empowers, teaches, convicts, and convinces you of events around you. Self-control is your ability to exercise great control over your free will. When you have great control of your free will, you do not carelessly express strong emotions or acting impulsively.

Self-control is also the ability to lead yourself effectively before leading others. No matter how gifted you are, without self-control you will achieve no sustainable impact. Exercising self-control helps to improve the quality of your spiritual and physical life. With self-control, you discipline yourself to make continuous progress towards your goal.

God does not discriminate. He can call a child or an adult depending on His purpose. God equips everyone with an assurance of victory. All you need to do is to hear God's call and respond appropriately. But in hearing and responding to God's call, you must be sensitive to know who a detractor is.

Powerful prayer point
Lack of self-control, you are fired out of my life now.

I encourage you to take these prayer declarations daily. Fervent prayer kicks a lack of self-control out of your life. Pray Now

Thank you, Lord, for counting me worthy to be among your elects. Please Lord, help me to stir up the spirit of self-control in my life.

1. I confess and repent of all my sins and I ask you, Lord, to come into my heart and renew a right spirit within me.
2. In the name of Jesus Christ, every lack of self-control you are fired out of my life now and forever.
3. Every evil spirit behind the lack of self-control in my life, knowingly and unknowingly; in the mighty name of Jesus Christ of Nazareth you are fired out now and forever. Amen.
4. I believe Jesus Christ died for my sins and He is alive in me. In that name that is above all names, Jesus Christ of Nazareth, I command every evil that oversees the lack of self-control in my life to die by fire and thunder.
5. Heavenly Father, destroy any attitude in me that gives up easily, in the mighty name of Jesus Christ.

6. Oh Lord, I reject an unproductive and self-defeating mind in the mighty name of Jesus Christ

7. Oh Lord, have mercy upon me for lack of self-control and disorganize every witchcraft altar that is influencing me to act contrary in life by fire, in the mighty name of Jesus Christ.

8. Arrow of lack of self-control attacking my life, in the name that is above all names, Jesus, be uprooted and scatter by fire and thunder.

9. Wind of lack of self-control blowing and circulating my life, what are you waiting for? Die by fire in the name of Jesus Christ.

10. Marine powers moving me against God's expectation for my life and destiny; wither and perish in the name of Jesus Christ.

11. Negative habits prevalent in my life, that is operating in my life

unknowingly; in the name that is above all names, Jesus, be uprooted and cut out from my life now by fire.

12. Holy Spirit, visit me by fire; I receive the power to control myself today and forever in Jesus' Name.

Three

You Are God's Divine Project

❦❦❦◆❦❦❦

F or thou hast possessed my reins: thou hast covered me in my mother's womb. I will praise thee; for I am fearfully and wonderfully made: marvellous are thy works; and that my soul knoweth right well. My substance was not hid from thee, when I was made in secret, and curiously wrought in the lowest parts of the

[48]

earth. Thine eyes did see my substance, yet being unperfect; and in thy book all my members were written, which in continuance were fashioned, when as yet there was none of them – Psalm 139:13-16 KJV.

You are God's divine project and His ambassador representing His Kingdom here on earth. You are the chosen generation, a royal priesthood, and a holy nation. The Word of God has revealed that you are unique, special, and a peculiar person in the sight of God. I want you to know that God has deposited something special in your life. As a result, Satan brings things that do not matter to distract you.

God designed you uniquely to fit into a special place on this earth. You have been given special features to help you accomplish special tasks in your generation. Everyone is created with a special talent for a special mission in His vineyard. What you are seeing now may be good in your sight, but God may desire that you see differently. God has chosen you to be conformed to the likeness of His beloved son Jesus Christ

An example of God's divine project is Saul who later became Apostle Paul.

"And Saul, yet breathing out threatenings and slaughter against the disciples of the Lord, went unto the high priest, And desired of him letters to Damascus to the synagogues, that if he found any of this way, whether they were men or women, he might bring them bound unto Jerusalem. And as he journeyed, he came near Damascus: and suddenly there shined round about him a light from heaven: And he fell to the earth, and heard a voice saying unto him, Saul, Saul, why persecutest thou me? And he said, Who art thou, Lord? And the Lord said, I am Jesus whom thou persecutest: it is hard for thee to kick against the pricks. And he trembling and astonished said, Lord, what wilt thou have me to do? And the

Lord said unto him, Arise, and go into the city,
and it shall be told thee what thou must do. And
the men which journeyed with him stood speechless,
hearing a voice, but seeing no man. And Saul
arose from the earth; and when his eyes were
opened, he saw no man: but they led him by the
hand, and brought him into Damascus. And he
was three days without sight, and neither did eat
nor drink. And there was a certain disciple at
Damascus, named Ananias; and to him said the
Lord in a vision, Ananias. And he said, Behold,
I am here, Lord. And the Lord said unto him,
Arise, and go into the street which is called
Straight, and enquire in the house of Judas for one
called Saul, of Tarsus: for, behold, he prayeth,
And hath seen in a vision a man named Ananias
coming in, and putting his hand on him, that he
might receive his sight. Then Ananias answered,
Lord, I have heard by many of this man, how
much evil he hath done to thy saints at Jerusalem:
And here he hath authority from the chief priests
to bind all that call on thy name. But the Lord
said unto him, Go thy way: for he is a chosen

vessel unto me, to bear my name before the Gentiles, and kings, and the children of Israel: For I will shew him how great things he must suffer for my name's sake. And Ananias went his way, and entered into the house; and putting his hands on him said, Brother Saul, the Lord, even Jesus, that appeared unto thee in the way as thou camest, hath sent me, that thou mightest receive thy sight, and be filled with the Holy Ghost. And immediately there fell from his eyes as it had been scales: and he received sight forthwith, and arose, and was baptized. And when he had received meat, he was strengthened. Then was Saul certain days with the disciples which were at Damascus. And straightway he preached Christ in the synagogues, that he is the Son of God," Acts 9:1-20.

Saul was a zealot persecuting the Church of Christ. God created him and defined his business as a chosen instrument for the Gentiles. Saul was destined to meet kings, preach the message to the people of Israel, and suffer for Jesus Christ. However, he was distracted and did contrary to his God-given purpose. Satan knows how to destroy a soul to stop it from becoming what God wants it to be. And some of the weapons he uses are:

Ignorance

Ignorance is when you do not have adequate knowledge, understanding, or information about something. If you do not know about something you cannot have value for it and if you are not determined to know it, you will remain ignorant. Satan fears those who know what God has deposited in them. When you fail to know who God is in your life, you will be ignorant of the power that God has invested in your life to accomplish your destiny. The devil will make you believe the lie that you are not fit for God's use. If you do not know, you will fall for the bait of the devil by looking down on yourself.

The problem with many today is that they have no strong desire for the Word of God. They are unable to gain the right kind of knowledge to fully understand what God has deposited in them.

What does the bible say about *ignorance*?

Acts 17:30-31 (ESV) says, *"The times of ignorance God overlooked, but now he commands all people everywhere to repent, because he has fixed a day on which he will judge the world in righteousness by a man whom he has appointed; and of this he has given assurance to all by raising him from the dead."*

Ephesians 4:18-19 says *"Having the understanding darkened, being alienated from the life of God through the ignorance that is in them, because of the blindness of their heart: Who being past feeling have given themselves over unto lasciviousness, to work all uncleanness with greediness."*

2 Corinthians 2:11 says *"Lest Satan should get an advantage of us: for we are not ignorant of his devices."*

Hosea 4:6 says *"My people are destroyed for lack of knowledge: because thou hast rejected knowledge, I will also reject thee, that thou shalt be no priest to me: seeing thou hast forgotten the law of thy God, I will also forget thy children."*

Acts 17:29-31 *"Forasmuch then as we are the offspring of God, we ought not to think that the Godhead is like unto gold, or silver, or stone, graven by art and man's device. And the times of this ignorance God winked at; but now commandeth all men every where to repent: Because he hath appointed a day, in the which he will judge the world in righteousness by that man whom he hath ordained; whereof he hath given assurance unto all men, in that he hath raised him from the dead."*

As God's divine project, what you need to do is to stand for Jesus Christ. This means that, you need to live and act in ways that support the gospel of our Lord and Savior Jesus Christ. Do everything possible to arm yourself with the true knowledge of God's Word. Ignorance is not an excuse for not fulfilling God's purpose for your life here on earth.

Benjamin Franklin says, "being ignorant is not so much a shame, as being unwilling to learn." Even Satan cannot stop you when you gain the knowledge of God's Word because you will have the power to subdue the work of the enemies.

Luke 10:19 says *"Behold, I give unto you power to tread on serpents and scorpions, and over all the power of the enemy: and nothing shall by any means hurt you."*

As Christians, we have been empowered by our Lord Jesus Christ to overcome the powers of the enemy. Anytime you stand up intelligently by faith through Jesus Christ, Satan falls because greater is He that in you than he that is in the world.

Fire at Satan and his demonic agents' bullets of prayer with praise and fasting. Do not respect or be gentle with them, do not negotiate with them that they may leave your life alone. Instead, command them in the name that is above all name, Jesus Christ of Nazareth whom you serve and believe, and shout leave me now. However, you can only command Satan when you are obedient to God. When you live by the examples of Christ, the devil will be afraid of you because he knows that the Greater One lives in you.

1 John 4:4 *"Ye are of God, little children, and have overcome them: because greater is he that is in you, than he that is in the world."* My prayer for you is that the knowledge of the Word of God will illuminate your life in the mighty name of Jesus Christ. I pray that the Lord will continue to open your spiritual eyes to his words as you meditate on it.

Sin

Sin is mentioned hundreds of times in the bible, starting with the *"original"* sin when Adam and Eve disobeyed God by eating the fruit from the tree of knowledge. Sin is a violation of God's laws, a transgression of God's principles. Christians and non-Christians rebelling against God's word are representatives of Lucifer here on earth because they do not love God wholeheartedly and not capable of obeying Him. I also see "sin" as a behavioral attitude that many people refuse to leave because it makes them feel good in the presence of other people.

There is no condemnation if you repent and accept Jesus Christ into your life genuinely. Jesus Christ has paid the price for you through His precious blood. All you need to do is agree with Him. As a child of God, you must quit acting righteous in the face of the world while violating God's commandments at the same time.

When you are conscious of sin you will be under a pressure to sin. Also, when you are conscious of righteousness as a believer you will become righteous. Righteousness can only be found through your faith in what Jesus Christ did on the Cross for us all. We are to act in the right way toward God by obeying His commandments. Also, you should be ready and willing to tell others about the benefits of obeying God's Word. As you share the gospel of Christ with others, the word of God roots deeper in you.

Nevertheless, we need to fire the spirit of sin from our life through prayer and engaging Kingdom principles to fulfill God's divine purpose for our lives. I believe that it is time for believers to re-examine their lives if they have truly confessed and repented from their sinful ways.

The Bible says *"If we claim to be without sin, we deceive ourselves and the truth is not in us. If we confess our sins, he is faithful and just and will forgive us our sins and purify us from all unrighteousness. If we claim we have not sinned, we make him out to be a liar and his word has no place in our lives,"* 1John 1:8-10 KJV.

Isaiah 59:1-2 says *"Behold, the LORD's hand is not shortened, that it cannot save; neither his ear heavy, that it cannot hear: But your iniquities have separated between you and your God, and your sins have hid his face from you, that he will not hear."*

If you are not fulfilling your destiny as the word of God has spoken concerning your life, you must examine your life to know if you are entangled in the web of sin. Sin reduces a great man to nothing. Sin is missing out on what God expects of you.

When you fall short of God's Word, you end up where you are not meant to be.

It is never late to make it up with Jesus Christ because you are still alive and reading this book. I also was once lost in the world of sin and I thought I was living right. Thanks to God for His grace that brought me back to His Word. He can do the same for you right now as you read this book. Do not postpone your freedom from the things that stall your relationship with God. Do not say that the grace of God is sufficient for you and continue in sin. Romans 6:1 *"What shall we say then? Shall we continue in sin, that grace may abound? God forbid. How shall we, that are dead to sin, live any longer therein?"* The grace of God is sufficient for us is to live above sin.

Bad association
For you to grow to maturity as a believer, you must choose godly friends who support you in your Christian journey.

Anyone who hates God should not be your friend. The word of God tells us in 2 Corinthians 6:14-15 that *"Be ye not unequally yoked together with unbelievers: for what fellowship hath righteousness with unrighteousness? and what communion hath light with darkness? And what concord hath Christ with Belial? or what part hath he that believeth with an infidel?"* There is a possibility that God can instruct you to relate with people who are opposed to Him. In such an exceptional situation, He will be doing that for His purpose. You must be sure that it is God that instructed you to go into association with ungodly people. For example, if God allows a Christian to marry an unbeliever, I believe that there is a purpose to it. The battle might be tough, but it will become a testimony eventually.

However, when someone tells you that disobedience to God or sinning doesn't matter and that all you need to do is to pray for forgiveness and continue to live recklessly, you should know that such a fellow should not be your friend. David says *"For they speak against thee wickedly, and thine enemies take thy name in vain. Do not I hate them, O LORD, that hate thee? and am not I grieved with those that rise up against thee? I hate them with perfect hatred: I count them mine enemies,"* Psalms 139:20-22 KJV.

God has chosen us to be conformed to the likeness of His begotten son. We are positioned to share God's inheritance through Jesus Christ.

"For those God foreknew he also predestined to be conformed to the image of his Son, that he might be the firstborn among many brothers and sisters. And those he predestined, he also called; those he called, he also justified those he justified, he also glorified," Romans 8:29-30 NIV.

Four

Grace to Accomplish Purpose

*W*ho is the image of the invisible God, the firstborn of every creature: For by him were all things created, that are in heaven, and that are in earth, visible and invisible, whether they be thrones, or dominions, or principalities, or powers: all things were created by *him, and for him: And he is before all things, and by him all things consist. And he is the head of the body, the church: who is the beginning, the firstborn from the dead; that in all things he might have the pre-eminence* – Colossians 1:15-18 NIV.

Every believer needs the Grace of God to fulfill his or her given assignment here on earth. Though we are living in a world where everyone has free will nevertheless, we must recognize our God as the one who is the greatest and sees through all. God knows the end from the beginning and the beginning from the end. For us to understand God's purpose for our lives, we must understand His reason for keeping us alive to this point.

Some of us are born into families of great wealth, prestige, and power to enjoy honors in society. But, when we receive Christ, we are born again and become a member of the Kingdom of God, full of love and grace to accomplish God's task. According to the Scriptures as in Romans 8:28 *"and we know that for those who love God all things work together for good, for those who are called according to his purpose,"* NIV.

When you fail to understand God's purpose for your life and situation, you are bound to fail in life. That all things work together for our good does not mean that all the bad and ugly is from God. God is not the author of sicknesses, divorces, accidents, broken relationships, and incurable diseases. Some of these life situations are the consequence of the choice that we make. They are from the devil. When you give your life to Jesus Christ, you will receive divine direction for daily living. By meditating on the word of God, you get a clear understanding of God's power. And the power living in you as a genuine believer of His Word becomes potent.

An eyewitness to the crucifixion of Jesus wrote that *"When Jesus had tasted it, He said, it is finished! He bowed His head and released His spirit"* John 19:30 NIV. This statement from Jesus Christ is not the cry of a defeated man but the shout of victory for believers. It is also an assurance to believers that they can call upon Him for solutions in their time of trouble. John Quincy Adams says, "patience and perseverance have a magical effect before which difficulties disappear and obstacles vanish."

Jesus Christ said it is finished and it means his redemptive work has been completed. Then, all the bad and ugly things will work together for your good because you genuinely love God and are walking according to His purpose for your life. But for the people of the world who despise the works of God and disobey His Word, a bad situation does not work for their good. The people of the world have no inheritance to hold onto in the Kingdom of God. When bad things happen to unbelievers, nothing changes for them except they return to God. The children of God tap into their inheritance in Christ and come out victorious even when bad things happen to them or around them.

I want you to know that God is not behind any unpleasant situation. Psalm 34:19 says, *"Many are the afflictions of the righteous: but the Lord delivereth him out of them all."* When the Word of God says that all things work together for good for those that love God and are called according to His purpose; it is describing who believers are and their inheritance, and not conditions for Christian living. Conditions for Christian living are fully expressed through the fruits of the Holy Spirit. Believers are those who love God because they know that God first loved them as emphasized in 1 John 4:19, *"We love Him, because He first loved us. And they are called according to His purpose for they have been born again, belong to Him and living a Holy and a righteous life."*

The moment you become a member of God's Kingdom by accepting Jesus into your life and you have been baptized by the Holy Spirit, all things will work for your good. This is your inheritance as a treasured child of God!

As a Christian who has a passion for accomplishing destiny, you need the Grace of God and it is also important to be committed to a lifelong pursuit of spiritual maturity. Spiritual growth begins at salvation when Jesus Christ sets you free from the chains of sin. It continues as you walk in this newness of life to remain free from the shackles of sin. Apostle Paul also addressed the importance of growing spiritually following his divine encounter with Jesus Christ.

In Romans 6:1-7, Apostle Paul writes that *"What shall we say then? Shall we continue in sin, that grace may abound? God forbid. How shall we, that are dead to sin, live any longer therein? Know ye not, that so many of us as were baptized into Jesus Christ were baptized into his death? Therefore we are buried with him by baptism into death: that like as Christ was raised up from the dead by the glory of the Father, even so, we also should walk in newness of life. For if we have been planted together in the likeness of his death, we shall be also in the likeness of his resurrection: Knowing this, that our old man is crucified with him, that the body of sin might be destroyed, that henceforth we should not serve sin. For he that is dead is freed from sin."*

What is grace?
Grace is the love of God shown to the ungodly; the peace of God given to the restless; and the unmerited favor of God to all. In Exodus 34:6-7, the Word of God says *"And the Lord passed by before him, and proclaimed, The Lord, The Lord God, merciful*

and gracious, longsuffering, and abundant in goodness and truth, keeping mercy for thousands, forgiving iniquity and transgression and sin, and that will by no means clear the guilty; visiting the iniquity of the fathers upon the children, and upon the children's children, unto the third and to the fourth generation." It is through Christ's sacrifice, His blood, that God gives us grace. Romans 3:24 says *"Being justified freely by His grace through the redemption that is in Christ Jesus."* It is through Christ that we receive God's grace; and if we did not receive that grace, we would die without accomplishing God's purpose.

Ephesians 1:3-6 says *"Blessed be the God and Father of our Lord Jesus Christ, who hath blessed us with all spiritual blessings in heavenly places in Christ: According as he hath chosen us in him before the foundation of the world, that we should be holy and without blame before him in love: Having predestinated us unto the adoption of children by Jesus Christ to himself, according to the good pleasure of his will, To the praise of the glory of his grace, wherein he hath made us accepted in the beloved."*

The Word of God has shown us that it is God's plan all along to be gracious to mankind. He did this by forgiving us of our sins and predestined us for an adoption and acceptance by Him. You are the beloved of God through Christ Jesus, and you have been given the grace to fulfill your divine calling.

Five

Discovering God's Divine Purpose

❧━━◦◦✦◦◦━━☙

*B*efore I formed you in the womb I knew you,
and before you were born I consecrated you;
I appointed you a prophet to the nations —
Jeremiah 1:5 NIV.

As revealed in the bible, God told the
prophet, Jeremiah, that He knew him even

before he was born. He (God) knows what Prophet Jeremiah is going to become and He endows and empowers him with the power and strength to achieve purpose even before he was born. As a child of God, you need to recognize who you are in God through Jesus Christ. You will discover God's divine purpose for your life the moment you surrender all to Jesus Christ.

(1) Divine purpose is when God's Word is glorified in your personal life.
(2) Divine purpose is when you allow God to take center stage in all things in your life.
(3) Divine purpose is when you understand grace by rejecting ungodliness and worldly possessions.
(4) Divine purpose is desiring the Lord so that He may purify you to live holy and righteously.

(5) Divine purpose is when you make God's will first in your life and nothing else.

How to discover your divine purpose

1. Build a prayer altar and fast regularly

Discovering your divine purpose requires building a prayer altar and fasting regularly. Prayer is important for everything as a Christian. Prayer is the master key to communicate with and receive from God. If you cannot pray you cannot receive from God. A prayerless Christian is a powerless Christian. Fasting gets you ready to receive from God. If you pray as you should, you will constantly be led by the Spirit of God. If you cannot pray and fast, you cannot be filled with the power of the Holy Spirit.

2. Meditate on the word of god day and night

Meditating on God's Word brings life to your vision and it gives you power and control over your actions. When you meditate on the Word of God, you are led to what God has prepared for you. If you do not meditate on God's Word, it will be difficult to know why God called you.

3. Discipline yourself physically and spiritually

A disciplined Christian has the capacity to grow to a place of maturity physically and spiritually. Physical discipline is organizing your physical activities in a way that the name of God is glorified in your life. Spiritual discipline is actively feeding your spirit and soul with godly contents to get you ready for heaven.

4. Have an enduring spirit

If I did not endure affliction, it may be difficult for me to say I am fulfilling God's purpose. It is by the virtue of endurance that I am able to achieve a lot in my marriage. Without enduring affliction, you will not achieve your purpose in life. Achieving purpose is not an easy task, but you need endurance to gain your crown.

5. Faith

Faith is the substance of things hoped for. You must have faith in God to fulfill your purpose when going through challenges. By faith, you go for what is not seen with the assurance that God is with you and will bring to manifestation His promises.

6. Have a relationship with god (being born again)

> You can only understand the importance of faith, endurance, prayers, and fasting to the fulfilment of your divine purpose if you have a relationship with God. Without a relationship with God you cannot have these virtues.

In Colossians 1:15-20, the Word of God says, *"Who is the image of the invisible God, the firstborn of every creature: For by him were all things created, that are in heaven, and that are in earth, visible and invisible, whether they be thrones, or dominions, or principalities, or powers: all things were created by him, and for him: And he is before all things, and by him all things consist. And he is the head of the body, the church: who is the beginning, the firstborn from the dead; that in all things he might have the pre-eminence. For it pleased the Father that in him should all fullness dwell; And, having made peace through the blood of his cross, by him to reconcile all things unto himself; by him, I say, whether they be things in earth, or things in heaven."*

Knowing God's divine purpose for your life enhances your understanding of service to God. Being a faithful follower of Christ through your role as a minister of the gospel of Jesus Christ brings you into the realm of perfection and preservation. In Jeremiah 1:5, *"the word of the Lord came unto Jeremiah saying before I God formed you in your mother's womb I knew you, and I have appointed you to speak for me on earth as my prophet, you will be my voice to the nations of the world."* Because Jeremiah did not understand what the Lord told him, in verse 6-7, he replied and said to God *"...Ah, Lord GOD! behold, I cannot speak: for I am a child. But the LORD said unto me, Say not, I am a child: for thou shalt go to all that I shall send thee, and whatsoever I command thee thou shalt speak."*

Until you discover God's divine purpose for your life, you will look down on yourself and underestimate the value God places on you. As a matter of fact, you will also keep the wrong people around you, follow the wrong kind of instructions and live wrongly. As it is for Prophet Jeremiah and other prophets in the bible, God has specific calling and task for you on earth to do. However, you must call upon God for direction and insights.

You need insights from the Word of God so that it illuminates your mind. With this understanding, you begin to run with the purpose of God for your life. In Jeremiah 1:8-19, the Word of God says *"Be not afraid of their faces: for I am with thee to deliver thee, saith the Lord. Then the Lord put forth his hand, and touched my mouth. And the Lord said unto me, Behold, I have put my words in thy mouth. See, I have this day set thee over the nations and the kingdoms, to root out, and to pull down, and to destroy, and to throw down, to build, and to plant. Moreover the word of the Lord came unto me, saying, Jeremiah, what seest thou? And I said, I see a rod of an almond tree. Then said the Lord unto me, Thou hast well seen: for I will hasten my word to perform it. And the word of the Lord came unto me the second time, saying, Whatseest thou? And I said, I see a seething pot; and the face thereof is toward the north. Then the Lord said unto me, Out of the north an evil shall break forth upon all the inhabitants of the land. For, lo, I will call all the families of the kingdoms of the north, saith the Lord; and they shall come, and they shall set every one his throne at the entering of the gates of Jerusalem, and against all the walls thereof round about, and against all the cities of Judah. And I will utter my judgments against them touching all their wickedness, who have forsaken me, and have burned incense unto other gods, and worshipped the works of their own hands. Thou therefore gird up thy loins, and arise, and speak unto them all that I command thee: be not dismayed at their faces, lest I confound thee before them. For, behold, I have made thee this day a defenced city, and an iron pillar, and brasen walls against the whole land, against the kings of Judah, against the princes thereof, against the priests thereof, and against the people of the land.*

And they shall fight against thee; but they shall not prevail against thee; for I am with thee, saith the Lord, to deliver thee."

As you read this book, what is Lord saying to you? What is the Holy Spirit ministering to you right now? What is your purpose? Is it to advance the Kingdom of God? How can the Kingdom of God be advanced through you? What are you doing to discover God's divine purpose for your life? What are you doing to deal with distractions? You must understand that before God can reveal to you your purpose in life you have to be committed to Him. God created you to advance His purpose for your life and He has endowed you with the gifts to achieve it. God does not neglect those He has called.

There is good news for you. Matthew 16:24-26 *"Then said Jesus unto his disciples, if any man will come after me, let him deny himself, and take up his cross, and follow me. For whosoever will save his life shall lose it: and whosoever will lose his life for my sake shall find it. For what is a man profited, if he shall gain the whole world, and lose his soul? or what shall a man give in exchange for his soul?"*

I encourage you to make the right choice to follow Jesus Christ in truth and spirit. By this, the consequence of sin and sorrow will be taken away from your life. As a Christian, you must live an obedient and Christ-honoring life before God. If you are disobedient, He will chasten you. *"For whom the Lord loveth he chasteneth, and scourgeth every son whom he receiveth. If ye endure chastening, God dealeth with you as with sons; for what son is he whom the father chasteneth not? But if ye be without chastisement, whereof all are partakers, then are ye bastards, and not sons. Furthermore we have had fathers of our flesh which corrected us, and we gave them reverence: shall we not much rather be in subjection unto the Father of spirits, and live? For they verily for a few days chastened us after their own pleasure; but he for our profit, that we might be partakers of his holiness. Now no chastening for the present seemeth to be joyous, but grievous: nevertheless afterward it yieldeth the peaceable fruit of righteousness unto them which are exercised thereby,"* Hebrews 12:6-11KJV.

You are salt of the earth

Matthew 5:13-16 says *"Ye are the salt of the earth: but if the salt have lost his savour, wherewith shall it be salted? it is thenceforth good for nothing, but to be cast out, and to be trodden under foot of men. Ye are the light of the world. A city that is set on a hill cannot be hid. Neither do men light a candle, and put it under a bushel, but on a candlestick; and it giveth light unto all that are in the house. Let your light so shine before men, that they may see your good works, and glorify your Father which is in heaven."*

Your presence here on earth as a child of God is to season somebody's life. Salt is a naturally occurring white substance used to season or preserve food. Job 6:6 says, *"Can that which is unsavoury be eaten without salt? or is there any taste in the white of an egg?"* When Jesus Christ was on earth, many lives were seasoned by the message He preached. His messages brought them healing and deliverance of all kinds. Jesus Christ of Nazareth did not only teach them the Word, but he also pleased His heavenly father.

I encourage you to live a life that will improve the lives of others just as salt makes food taste better. If you are a committed Christian, your life should provide an example of the relationship that should exist between God and man to unbelievers. Therefore, a Christian work for the Kingdom of God should be tasteful and not tasteless. The work of a Christian becomes tasteless when he refuses to do the will of God. I pray that you will be remembered as a salt that seasons the lives of others for God's glory. I command the power of God from above to fall upon you and destroy what distracts you from being a "salt" of the earth.

Sadly, some believers and leaders of the gospel have turned their salt to insult. Instead of being a tasteful seasoning for Jesus through righteousness and holy living, they are now insulting the body of Christ by destroying the finished work of Grace. They have turned grace into disgrace because of their selfish ambition. God commits to what is good and rejects what is evil. His fury and wrath are not like in humans but a wave of Holy anger against sin. Even as God directs His fury against evil, He continues to offer His mercy to all who will turn from their sin.

God wants every soul to be saved, and He takes no pleasure in a sinner's death. Ezekiel 33:11 says *"Say unto them, As I live, saith the Lord God, I have no pleasure in the death of the wicked; but that the wicked turn from his way and live: turn ye, turn ye from your evil ways; for why will ye die, O house of Israel?".* In His mercy, He patiently waits for everyone to repent and turn from our sinful ways. God is slow to anger, so we have an opportunity to turn away from our sin before He sends His judgment.

Although, people seem to have the false impression that they are immune to the realities of life because God is slow to anger. This is a dangerous way to live and serve God.

God who has called and commissioned us will equip and empower us to accomplish the task of soulwinning. All you need is to be filled with the Holy Spirit and your knowledge of the Word of God. Be zealous for soul winning and pray to break barriers and obstacles. Romans 10:1 says, *"Brethren, my heart's desire and prayer to God for Israel is, that they might be saved."*

You are light to the world

Jesus Christ said you are light to this world, and He expects us to walk in that light. 1 John 1:5-7 says *"This then is the message which we have heard of him, and declare unto you, that God is light, and in him is no darkness at all. If we say that we have fellowship with him, and walk-in darkness, we lie and do not the truth: But if we walk in the light, as he is in the light, we have fellowship one with another, and the blood of Jesus Christ his Son cleanseth us from all sin."*

In this verse, John the beloved of Jesus Christ wants to portray to us a picture of God as light, *"God is light and in him is no darkness at all."* It means that if you draw near to God, you will find deliverance, joy, peace, and forgiveness. You will find illumination.

The world today is covered with so much darkness and troubles because millions are making the wrong choice daily by sinning.

God has provided a way out through Jesus Christ who paid the price for us more than 2000 years ago. What is holding millions back from this light is their refusal to take advantage of the sacrifice of Jesus Christ for their redemption.

Sin is what enters your life through your wrong choice and that which you do not want to let go because it tastes good to your flesh. The book of 1 John 1: 8-10 says, *"If we say that we have no sin, we deceive ourselves and the truth is not in us. If we confess our sins, He is faithful and just to forgive us our sins, and to cleanse us from all unrighteousness. If we say that we have not sinned, we make Him a liar, and His Word is not in us."*

The bible also tells us in John 8:12 *"Then spake Jesus again unto them saying, I am the light of the world: he that followeth me shall not walk in darkness, but shall have the light of life."* The ability to overcome and shine as light gives us the ultimate assurance that we will never be separated from God. It is a place where there is no sorrow, pain, tears, and death. It is a place where there is no darkness because the glory of God shines perpetually. So, as a light in this dark world, you need to know the truth that liberates one from the stronghold of darkness.

How can you go about moving from darkness to light? You must tell Satan that he cannot quench your light. Satan will try to send different arrows to attack you and to put your light off. Satan will use discouragement and self-pity to attack your life. Satan will incite you with fleshly desires through your unbelieving spirit.

Satan can physically afflict you with illness, disasters, persecution - because he wants you to doubt the power of the mighty God. The major channel Satan uses to attack Christian is unbelief and he does this by attacking your mind. *"Ye are of your father the devil and the lusts of your father ye will do. He was a murderer from the beginning, and abode not in the truth, because there is no truth in him. When he speaketh a lie, he speaketh of his own: for he is a liar and the father of it,"* John 8:44 KJV.

Satan is by nature a liar and his primary method with which he attacks is through lies to deceive people into believing falsehood about God. Satan attempts to make believers think God's plan is not good for them and stirs rebellion. Satan lies about who God is, what God is like, what you are, God's desires for you, and how to be saved.

Whenever you find yourself complaining about what God has not done instead of thanksgiving, you will know that this is a sign that you are being attacked by the enemy. Satan spreads lies about God through worldly wisdom. Satan does this because he wants to destroy your desire to live a holy life. Satan is neither omnipotent nor omniscient, but he has tremendous power of manipulation. The bible says, *"And we know that we are of God, and the whole world lieth in wickedness," I John 5:19.* His sword of craftiness is wielded in the time and space container in which we dwell.

Signs of satanic attacks

1. Anytime your faith in Jesus Christ begins to grow weak as a Christian, just know that Satan is attacking or fighting your light.
2. Whenever you are too busy to read your bible or spend quality time in the presence of God, Satan is about to capture you with a lie.
3. Whenever you begin to murmur because you experience a delay in the manifestation of God's promise for your life, then know your candlelight is under siege.

How to overcome satanic attacks

The bible says to us that *"Wherefore take unto you the whole amour of God, that you may be able to withstand in the evil day, and having done all, to stand. Stand therefore, having on the breastplate of righteousness; and your feet shod with the preparation of the gospel of peace; Above all, taking the shield of faith, wherewith you shall be able to quench all the fiery darts of the wicked. And take the helmet of salvation, and the sword of the Spirit, which is the word of God,"* Ephesians 6:13-17.

Anytime you demonstrate faith by relying on God's direction, your victory is guaranteed over the enemy. Ephesians 6:16 says *"Above all, taking the shield of faith, where with ye shall able to quench all the fiery darts of the wicked"*. The wicked one is Satan. You must not allow him to quench the light of God in you, and the light of faith given to you by God through His son Jesus Christ of Nazareth. John 5:4 says, *"For whatsoever is born of God overcometh the world: and this is the victory that overcometh the world, even our faith."*

Luke 10:38-42 (ESV) gives a clearer understanding of how important our commitment should be to Jesus. *"Now as they went on their way, Jesus entered a village. And a woman named Martha welcomed him into her house. And she had a sister called Mary, who sat at the Lord's feet and listened to his teaching. But Martha was distracted with much serving. And she went up to him and said, "Lord, do you not care that my sister has left me to serve alone? Tell her then to help me." But the Lord answered her, "Martha, Martha, you are anxious and troubled about many things, but one thing is necessary. Mary has chosen the good portion, which will not be taken away from her."* Jesus Christ needs our full attention and He wants us to change our attitude in accordance with the Word of God. This is because the Word of God has powerful elements that you need to destroy your enemy. Hebrews 4: 12 *"For the word of God is quick, and powerful, and sharper than any two-edged sword, piercing even to the dividing asunder of soul and spirit, and the joints and marrow, and is a discerner of the thoughts and intents of the heart."*

Jeremiah 23:29 (KJV) "Is not my word like as a fire? saith the Lord; and like a hammer that breaketh the rock in pieces?"

As you remain focused on God's Word, I prophesy into your life:

1. From this moment, you will receive a complete deliverance from the effects of evil foundations, in the mighty name of Jesus Christ.
2. I pray that blood of Jesus Christ of Nazareth will uproot every sin in your life, in the mighty name of Jesus Christ.
3. I declare and decree that from this moment onward, you will discover your divine purpose in life. And a new foundation shall be built for

you, in the mighty name of Jesus Christ.

4. I declare into your life with the power of Jehovah God. From henceforth, your life shall fulfill the five-fold creational blessings; you shall be fruitful, and you shall multiply. You shall subdue your environment and you will exercise unlimited dominion in every area of your life, in the mighty name of Jesus Christ.

5. I decree and declare that the sword of deliverance will cut down the tree of affliction and return it to the sender, in the mighty name of Jesus Christ.

Living a life of purpose

Six

Acting to Fulfill God's Purpose for Your Life

*F*ight the good fight of the faith. Take hold of the eternal life to which you were called when you made your good confession in the presence of many witnesses – 1Timothy 6:12 NIV.

There are so many things that destroy destinies and Satan is at the head of it all. I want you to understand that we are living in the days the Bible identifies as the perilous times. I want you to also understand that this is the time evil attempts to prevail over good. Everything that happens in the world is made to work according to God's purpose. The existence of evil is Satan's ploy to thwart God's plan. God uses even sinful men for His purposes because the bible says *"The king's heart is in the hand of the Lord, as the rivers of water: he turneth it whithersoever he will,"* Proverbs 21:1. Exodus 12:36 says *"And the Lord gave the people favour in the sight of the Egyptians, so that they lent unto them such things as they required. And they spoiled the Egyptians."* God worked on the hearts of the Egyptians to bring about His purpose.

Even when man's intent is purely evil, God can still bring about His will. However, you must understand warfare and authority. Warfare is waging war against an enemy. As a believer, you have been given the authority to speak and cause things to happen. You have been given authority as a child of God and you must know how to walk in it.

How to know you have been given power and authority

When you accept Jesus Christ as your Lord and Savior, you understand that you are His representative on earth. You are Jesus' representative on this earth right now if you are a born-again believer!

Colossians 1:13 says that *"Who hath delivered us from the power of darkness, and hath translated us into the kingdom of his dear Son."* The word power is translated "authority." You and I have been delivered from the authority of darkness and placed into God's Kingdom. This world and the king of this world, Satan, have no authority over you because through the redemptive power of Jesus Christ on the Cross of

Calvary you have been delivered from death.

Jesus said in Matthew 28:18-19 *"And Jesus came and spake unto them, saying, All power is given unto me in heaven and in earth. Go ye therefore, and teach all nations, baptizing them in the name of the Father, and of the Son, and of the Holy Ghost."* Power is given to you as part of your inheritance in Christ Jesus. You have the right to enter this position of authority because you are in Him.

Since the fall of Lucifer, there has been a war here on earth. Jesus Christ succeeded in securing all power by going to the Cross to die. He went down to the pit of hell to defeat Satan and He arose on the third day victorious. Whatever that has been stolen from you be it your health, finances, relationships by Satan will be restored to you, in the mighty name of Jesus Christ. Hindrances to your destiny fulfillment have been removed from your life, in the name of Jesus.

Haman tried to hinder Mordecai from taking his crown of honor, but he failed. Your enemy will not succeed over you, in the name of Jesus Christ. For everything that the devil stole from you, it is your responsibility to take authority and recover them all.

Apostle Paul writes in 2 Corinthians 10:1-11 *"Now I Paul myself beseech you by the meekness and gentleness of Christ, who in presence am base among you, but being absent am bold toward you: But I beseech you, that I may not be bold when I am present with that confidence, wherewith I think to be bold against some, which think of us as if we walked according to the flesh. For though we walk in the flesh, we do not war after the flesh – for the weapons of our warfare are not carnal, but mighty through God to the pulling down of strongholds – casting down imaginations, and every high thing that exalteth itself against the knowledge of God, and bringing into captivity every thought to the obedience of Christ; And having in a readiness to revenge all disobedience, when your obedience is fulfilled. Do ye look on things after the outward appearance? if any man trust to himself that he is Christ's, let him of himself think this again, that, as he is Christ's, even so, are we Christ's. For though I should boast somewhat more of our authority, which the Lord hath given us for edification, and not for your destruction, I should not be ashamed: That I may not seem as if I would terrify you by letters. For his letters, say they, are weighty and powerful; but his bodily presence is weak, and his speech contemptible. Let such a one think this, that, such as we are in word by letters when we are absent, such will we be also in deed when we are present."*

The name of Jesus is a weapon to use to enforce Satan's defeat. Satan is aware that he has been defeated but confuses you with fear so that you will not know the power and authority you have been given. He wants you to look at your circumstance and not trust the Word of God to come through for you. Satan wants to keep you from reading the bible and attending faith uplifting services. He knows that when you fellowship with other children of God, you will gain a deeper knowledge of the promises of God and apply it to your situation.

Declare these prophetic prayers:

1. Every environmental Pharaoh operating around me, die in the Red Sea, in the mighty name of Jesus Christ.
2. Every man contesting against the oil on my head, lose your power and die, in the mighty name of Jesus Christ.
3. Covenant oil of God fall upon me, in the mighty name of Jesus Christ.

Living a life of purpose

Seven

Crushing Conspirators

*A**nd from the days of John the Baptist until now the kingdom of heaven suffereth violence, and the violent take it by force –* Matthew 11:12.

Apostle Paul says in Ephesians 6:12 *"For we wrestle not against flesh and blood, but against principalities, against powers, against the rulers of the darkness of this world, against spiritual wickedness in high places."* God has equipped us with the right kind of spiritual amour to fight our battles. We are to wage war against principalities, powers of darkness, and spiritual wickedness in high places. You must understand the importance of calling on God for help and strength before engaging in spiritual warfare.

It is the will of God that His children always call on Him. When you call on God, it gives Him great pleasure that you are ready to communicate with Him through prayer. When you pray, believe in your heart that you are not communing with a dead god, but with a God that hears and answers prayer all the time. He will deliver you and show you His power and mercy.

In Jeremiah 33:3, the Word of God says *"Call unto me, and I will answer thee, and show thee great and mighty things, which thou knowestnot."* Do not allow conspirators to distract you because their mission is to kill, distract, and destroy without remorse.

Strategies of conspirators

1. To distract

When the enemy distracts you, they intend to shift your focus from God and His purpose for your life. The enemy may even use what you are familiar with to distract you.

2. To kill

The enemy may decide to kill your purpose by killing you spiritually so that you are unable to pray, study the word of God, and engage in fasting. When the enemy kills, it is to take you into captivity.

3. To destroy

When a person has been distracted and killed by the enemy, he is destroyed so that he is not redeemable.

Examples of conspiracies

Jesus delivered to Pilate

"When morning came, all the chief priests and the elders of the people took counsel against Jesus to put him to death," Matthew 27:1 EVS.

A plot to kill Paul

The bible says *"When it was day, the Jews made a plot and bound themselves by an oath neither to eat nor drink till they had killed Paul. There were more than forty who made this conspiracy. They went to the chief priests and elders and said, "We have strictly bound ourselves by an oath to taste no food till we have killed Paul. Now therefore you, along with the council, give notice to the tribune to bring him down to you, as though you were going to determine his case more exactly. And we are ready to kill him before he comes near,"* Acts 23:12-15 ESV.

Plot against Daniel

"Then the high officials and the satraps sought to find a ground for complaint against Daniel with regard to the kingdom, but they could find no ground for complaint or any fault, because he was faithful, and no error or fault was found in him. Then these men said, "We shall not find any ground for complaint against this Daniel unless we find it in connection with the law of his God." Then these high officials and satraps came by agreement to the king and said to him, "O King Darius, live forever! All the high officials of the kingdom, the prefects and the satraps, the counselors and the governors are agreed that the king should establish an ordinance and enforce an injunction, that whoever makes petition to any god or man for thirty days, except to you, O king, shall be cast into the den of lions. Now, O king, establish the injunction and sign the document, so that it cannot be changed, according to the law of the Medes and the Persians, which cannot be revoked. Therefore King Darius signed the document and injunction. When Daniel knew that

the document had been signed, he went to his house where he had windows in his upper chamber open toward Jerusalem. He got down on his knees three times a day and prayed and gave thanks before his God, as he had done previously. Then these men came by agreement and found Daniel making petition and plea before his God. Then they came near and said before the king, concerning the injunction, O king! Did you not sign an injunction, that anyone who makes petition to any god or man within thirty days except to you, O king, shall be cast into the den of lions? The king answered and said, The thing stands fast, according to the law of the Medes and Persians, which cannot be revoked." Then they answered and said before the king, Daniel, who is one of the exiles from Judah, pays no attention to you, O king, or the injunction you have signed, but makes his petition three times a day. Then the king, when he heard these words, was much distressed and set his mind to deliver Daniel. And he labored till the sun went down to rescue him. Then these men came by agreement to the king and said to the king, Know, O king, that it is a law of the Medes and Persians that no injunction or ordinance that the king establishes can be changed. Then the king commanded, and Daniel was brought and cast into the den of lions. The king declared to Daniel, "May your God, whom you serve continually, deliver you!" And a stone was brought and laid on the mouth of the den, and the king sealed it with his own signet and with the signet of his lords, that nothing might be changed concerning Daniel," Daniel 6:4-17 ESV.

No conspiracy can succeed against the plans and counsel of God concerning your life and destiny. For instance, Absalom conspired to overthrow David. It was a large and carefully planned conspiracy guided by the wise and crafty Ahitophel as contained in 2 Samuel 15:12 (NKJV), *"Then Absalom sent for Ahithophel the Gilonite, David's counselor, from his city, from Giloh; while he offered sacrifices. And the conspiracy grew strong, for the people with Absalom continually increased in number."* Conspiracies are dangerous and lead to civil unrest and strife as Absalom certainly did. They can even attempt to kill the righteous - as they did with Jesus Christ. But in the end, the plans of the conspirators come to nothing over the children of God.

Eight

Prayer Points to Deal with Distractors and Conspirators

───── ∞∾⌒❖⌒∾∞ ─────

*T*he kings of the earth set themselves, and the rulers take counsel together, against the Lord and against his Anointed, saying, Let us burst their bonds apart and cast away their cords from us. He who sits in the heavens laughs;

the Lord holds them in derision – Psalm 2:2 (ESV)

Ephesians 6:12 (KJV) says *"For we wrestle not against flesh and blood, but against principalities, against powers, against the rulers of the darkness of this world, against spiritual wickedness in high places."*

Ephesians 6:18 (AMP) says *"With all prayer and petition pray [with specific requests] at all times [on every occasion and in every season] in the Spirit, and with this in view, stay alert with all perseverance and petition [interceding in prayer] for all God's people"*

1 Thessalonians 5:16-18 (ESV) says *"Rejoice always, pray without ceasing, give thanks in all circumstances; for this is the will of God in Christ Jesus for you."*

Prayer points

1. Give God thanks because of His redemptive power which neither fails nor diminishes. Thank God for

the gift of life and the sustaining power at work in you.

2. Give God thanks and praise for His grace and truth that is alive to strengthen you even amid conspirators.

3. Give God thanks for the Holy Spirit that is present around you now, in the mighty name of Jesus Christ.

4. Give thanks to God for His mighty hands upon your life to fulfill His divine purpose here on earth.

5. Give God all the praise and worship for turning the counsel of the enemy into foolishness in your life and destiny.

Prophetic declarations

1. Lord, please walk back to the foundation of my life and carry out the necessary surgical operation by fire and thunder in the mighty name of Jesus Christ.

2. Holy Ghost fire burn from the top of my head to the sole of my feet, so that the enemy will not be able to reach or touch me in the mighty name of Jesus Christ.

3. I plead the blood of Jesus Christ of Nazareth over the spirit that does not want to let me go; and I command my deliverance now in the might name of Jesus Christ.

4. I arrest spiritual attackers and paralyze their activities in my life the mighty name of Jesus Christ.

5. Holy Ghost, cause a revival in my life and grant me the grace to live like Jesus all the days of my life.

6. I command every evil odor sent into my life to be neutralized now in the mighty name of Jesus Christ.

7. Lord God Almighty, you showed Joseph his throne, but not his thorns. My Father God, do the same for me. Send me a special

encouragement in the name of Jesus Christ.

8. God let anti-breakthrough designs against my life and destiny be shattered to irreparable pieces, in the mighty name of Jesus Christ.

9. I trample upon every enemy of my advancement and promotion, in the mighty name of Jesus Christ.

10. I cancel anything representing me in the demonic world against my destiny; be destroyed by the fire of God, in the mighty name of Jesus Christ.

11. Every ancestral curse working against my destiny and God's divine purpose for my life, what are you waiting for? Die now! In the mighty name of Jesus Christ.

12. Lord, in the presence of those who are asking for my God, oh God arise and manifest Yourself concerning Your divine purpose for

my life and destiny in the mighty name of Jesus Christ.

13. Every power, planning to wage war against my divine vision, blessing, and success; what are you waiting for? I command you to die now in the mighty name of Jesus Christ.

14. Every power that is refusing to let me go, what are you waiting for? Enough is enough for you, die, in the mighty name of Jesus Christ.

15. I command the satanic agenda against the purpose of God for my life to be demolished in the mighty name of Jesus Christ.

16. By the prophetic prayer of faith, I forcefully enter God's given inheritance in the mighty name of Jesus Christ of Nazareth.

17. I released myself from any collective captivity of destiny in the mighty name of Jesus Christ.

18. Every evil foundation supporting my enemies against me is destroyed. Enough is enough, die by fire and thunder, in the mighty name of Jesus Christ.

19. Every collective arrow fired against me and my divine destiny, return to your sender now by the fire of the Holy Ghost with double shame, in the Mighty name of Jesus Christ of Nazareth.

20. With the power of My Jehovah God, I break the unity of my enemies, in the name of Jesus. The blood of Jesus Christ stands against evil plans of the wicked concerning my life in the mighty name of Jesus Christ.

21. Every wicked proposal against me is canceled with the blood of Jesus Christ. Lord, give me the ability to handle all situations in Jesus' name.

22. Anything stolen or taken from me by evil forces is restored in Jesus' name. Any man or woman consulting evil powers to work against my destiny is paralyzed now in the mighty name of Jesus Christ.

23. Every conspiracy of the wicked strategy of the wicked against my life and destiny is scattered with frustration in the mighty name of Jesus Christ.

24. Every evil messenger assigned to pull me down. What are you waiting for? Die by thunder and by fire now, in the Mighty name of Jesus Christ.

25. Wicked association, you are fired from my life forever, in the mighty name of Jesus Christ. Amen.

26. Every war shouts or cries against me not to fulfill my destiny is shattered now by fire in Jesus' name.

27. Every organized battle against my life and vision, I command you to scatter, in the mighty name of Jesus Christ.
28. May the hostility of the enemy destroy them by fire and thunder, in the mighty name of Jesus Christ.
29. Every dark force against my life and destiny catch fire, in Jesus' name.
30. Oh Lord, destroy enemy intention towards me by fire by thunder in the mighty name of Jesus Christ
31. Every gang up to frustrate God's divine plans for my life, scatter in the name of Jesus Christ.
32. I fire an arrow of misunderstanding into the camp of the enemy. And I command Holy Ghost fire to destroy you and your agent now, in Jesus' name.
33. Satanic power plotting against me shall not succeed in Jesus' name.

34. Every covenant of the enemy with me is broken in Jesus' name.

35. Arrows of shame return to your sender in Jesus' name.

36. Arrows of disappointment return to your sender in Jesus' name.

37. Arrows of poverty and bewitchment fired into my life return to your sender in the mighty name of Jesus Christ.

38. Every altar of darkness speaking disappointment into my life, shut up in Jesus' name.

39. Any altar of darkness having my name on it, catch fire in Jesus name.

40. Every evil tongue, speaking against me, wither in Jesus' name.

41. Every occult gathering against me and my destiny. What are you waiting for? Scatter and die, in the mighty name of Jesus Christ.

42. I disconnect myself from every ancestral covenant, evil altar, and

satanic foundation holding my progress and fruitfulness in the mighty name of Jesus Christ.

43. God, thank You for putting end to the wickedness of the wicked concerning my life and destiny, in the mighty name of Jesus Christ.

44. God, I give you all the glory and honor for my prayer and the prophetic declarations You have answered in the mighty name of Jesus Christ.

Conclusion

God has a great plan for all His children including you. However, you must see life as a journey. And you are responsible for writing the story of your life. For you to tell a good story in life and beyond, you need to eliminate from your life anything that will distract you from fulfilling your God's given purpose. As children of the living God, you must withdraw yourself from the crowd and pray that God helps you to remain obedient to Him.

The word of God in Luke 22: 41-44(KJV) shares how Jesus leaves the crowd to seek the face of God. *"And he was withdrawn from them about a stone's cast, and kneeled down, and prayed, Saying, Father, if thou be willing, remove this cup from me: nevertheless not my will, but thine, be done. And there appeared an angel unto him from heaven, strengthening him. And being in an agony he prayed more earnestly: and his sweat was as it were great drops of blood falling down to the ground."* Luke 22:41-44 (KJV)

I encourage you to withdraw yourself from what keeps you away from the presence of the Almighty God. It is in Him you can get divine guidance and fulfillment of purpose. Ask God to help you become fervent in the place of prayer. When you master this important element of your spiritual growth, you will be unstoppable.

As you have more genuine communication with God through the leading of the Holy Spirit, you will be empowered with all the spiritual gifts needed to fulfill your destiny. And you will become an overcomer in life in Jesus' name. Amen!

About the book

I n this transformative book, Roseline Uwaifo tries to show why many people fail to achieve God's purpose for their lives. Using her life's experiences, she shows how she has been able to live a life of purpose. One important question she attempts to answer is: What is God's purpose for my life?

In response to this question, she shows that the purpose of God concerning mankind is to serve Him; and achieving this purpose is tied to fulfilling one's divine destiny. But it is important that man understands the role of the enemy, Satan, in derailing and distracting him from fulfilling purpose. The devil uses detractors to shift the focus of man from God. And a man who has lost his focus on God lacks confidence and can easily be beaten down by the enemy.

With reference to powerful Scriptures, Prophetess Uwaifo recommends actionable steps and powerful prayer points to deal with distractions and detractors.

Beautifully written and structured, *Living a Life of Purpose,* is definitely a reference guide that will impact your life for a very long time.

About author

ROSELINE UWAIFO is the Pastor of New Life in Christ Evangelical Ministry (The New Jerusalem), Westhoughton Bolton, United Kingdom. She has a prophetic anointing to speak the Word of God and to heal the broken-hearted.

Prophetess Roseline Uwaifo has a divine mandate to bring the message of hope, deliverance, and God's love to humanity through outreach services for children and the youth, widows and orphans, hospital patients and prison inmates.

Roseline Uwaifo is also a business administrator, a coach with Master of Science in Human Resources Management and Development (University of Salford, UK), B.Sc. (Hons) in Business Information Systems, (University of Bolton, UK), and a Diploma in Statistics (Auchi Polytechnic, Nigeria).

She founded the RosBeckley Foundation to support widows and orphans in Africa with the supply of basic needs. The foundation is financed with proceeds from her writing ministry.

She was married to the late Mr.Osahon Uwaifo and they are blessed with two children named Angel and Godswill.

References

1. Michael Barry, *The Forgiveness Project: The Startling Discovery of How to Overcome Cancer, Find Health, and Achieve Peace,* December 22, 2010

2. Joyce Meyer, web article available at *https://everydaystudy.joycemeyer.org/content/*

3. John Quincy Adams, web article available   at https://www.passiton.com/inspirational-quotes/3016-patience-and-perseverance-have-a-magical-effect

4. Web   article   available   at https://dailytimes.com.pk/287995/forgive-and-forget/

Living a life of purpose

Other books by Author

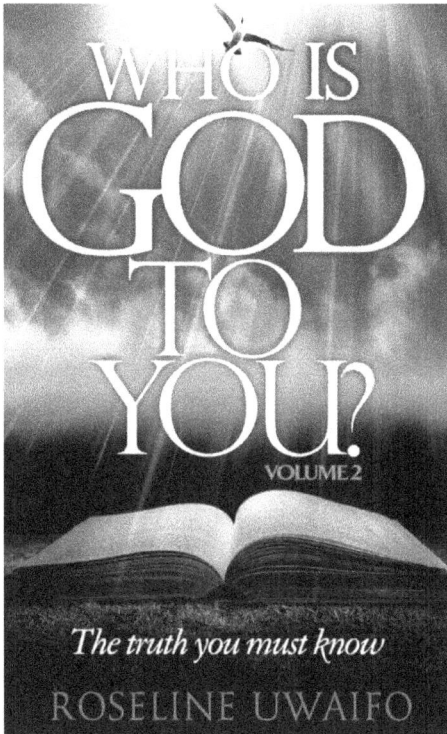

You can purchase a copy on Amazon at
https://www.amazon.co.uk/dp/B087YMZSHN

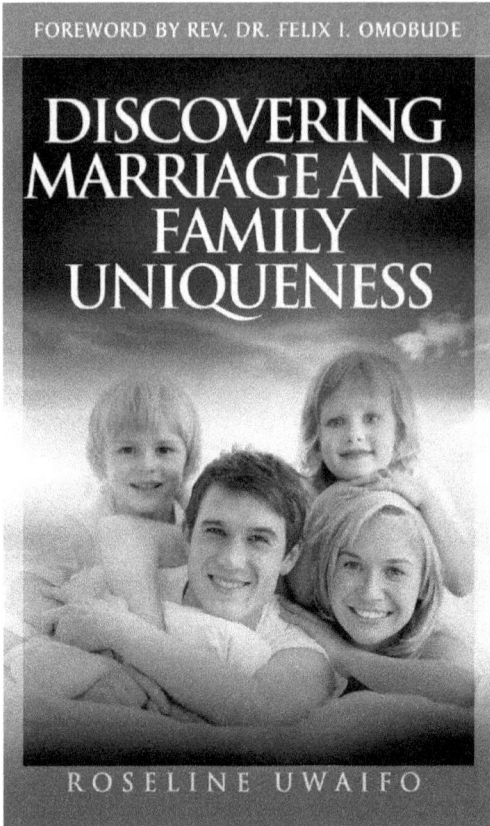

You can purchase a copy on Amazon at
https://www.amazon.co.uk/dp/B087PG5B7S

www.ingramcontent.com/pod-product-compliance
Lightning Source LLC
LaVergne TN
LVHW011353080426
835511LV00005B/279